New Moon

A Collection of Lessons and Wisdom

Alaya Daniel

New Moon copyright © 2019 by Alaya Daniel. All Rights Reserved. Printed in the United States of America. No part of this book may be used or reproduced by any means, graphic, electronic, or mechanical, including photocopying, recording, taping, or by any information storage retrieval system without the written permission of the publisher except in the case of brief quotations embodied in critical articles and reviews.

Kindle Direct Publishing
kdp.amazon.com

ISBN: 978-1-0873-7374-4

Editors: GermaNa Peoples & Anthony Banks
Book Cover Designer: Fadipe Isaac Olakanmi
Illustrator: Iqzan Saputra
Proofreader: Shaye Burnham

Author website: alayadaniel.com
Author Instagram: @alaya.daniel

To my husband who has supported me relentlessly since we were just 16. To my sisters who have known me longer and better than anyone. To my parents who have helped me to be the human that I am today.

Full Moon

2

Both brilliant and visible. I can finally see myself this way.

Nice People

Everyone assumes that
Nice people are delicate
Little flowers who constantly
Spit out smiles into the universe,
Dream of unicorns in greens fields
Accessorized by blue skies,
As they drink chamomile tea
And sit beneath the shade of a willow tree.

They have not a crooked bone in their body.
Their heart is generous,
Their love is plentiful
Even to parasitic souls who have
No other source of kindness.

Everyone assumes that nice people
Want to converse.
That they want you to pour all of your
Inconsistencies, problematic tendencies
And indecisive behavior,
Into their ears —
Only for them to spew out a brilliant solution
To all your madness.

Nice people are tired of your shit.

They are not walking diaries
Not should you treat them like one.
They have feelings that deserve expression
Despite perhaps your initial impression of them.
They are strong —

For those of you who have confused "nice" as a weak trait.
Because they have the ability to view the world through
A set of lenses that constantly smooth smudges
And repair its own cracks.
Nice people are B R A V E.
They are the only ones who still have the balls to be affectionate
Inside of a world that advises you to suppress your emotions.
Inside of a world that tells you to
"Get up, brush yourself off and stop being a bitch."
Nice people are R E S I L I E N T.
Untainted by the savagery and deceit of others.
They hold their composure like the Statue of Liberty grips her fiery torch
They are on fire.
Lighting up a room of gloom and a heart of sadness.

We do not value nice people enough.
We are so strung out on the expectation that people should be nice
And have forgotten that…
They don't have to be.

Learning the Power of My Voice

The summer before 9th grade is when I made a breakthrough. I decided that I no longer wanted to be known as the "quiet girl." Why? Because quiet girls get "tried," since everyone assumes that they have no backbone. Because quiet girls are overlooked, since no one ever hears them. Because quiet was a label that didn't coincide with all of the outrageous thoughts, ideas and opinions that raced through my mind, begging to be spoken.

I cannot remember the name of the book that I read that summer before 9th grade but I promise it was life-changing. The book was about how to become a more confident person and how emit that confidence. Before this summer, I was aware of the confidence that I was lacking which caused me to be quiet in situations where I otherwise wouldn't be. Like raising my hand in class when I had a question or speaking up when I had an opinion during group projects. While I wasn't looking to change my nature, I was looking to become equipped with a tool that I knew I would need for a lifetime – confidence in my voice.

Before the start of 9th grade I made gradual changes with my body language. When I walked into grocery stores or places of business, I made it a point to hold my head high and make subtle eye contact with strangers. While this may seem like a small thing, before this, I would walk into buildings with my eyes pointed at the ground, looking up occasionally, only to be sure not to bump into foreign objects. So, this was a huge step in my book. I even went as far as to make small talk with cashiers at checkout. Slowly I was preparing to show up with this sort of confidence in the most important place at this time in my life – high school. I understood that confident body language would reaffirm the confidence that I was nurturing for using my voice.

It was at this point in my life that I began to understand how valid my perspective and opinions are. Up until then I was timid and believed that I should be quiet, because no one wanted to hear about what I had to say anyway. I wasn't shy because I didn't *want* to talk to people. I was surprisingly eager and hopeful. I was shy because I lacked self-esteem. I had a few extroverted friends, and when I wasn't with them or my family, I was silent. Being around my extroverted friends who were outwardly themselves gave me permission to do the same. They've taught me that there is no shame in expressing how you feel, who you are and what you stand for. Being around family was another safe space that included ample conversation. My sisters and I would have conversations with my dad for hours at the kitchen table or outside on the front porch. Thoughts and ideas were always abundant in our household and especially always shared.

Outside of the safe spaces, my "quiet girl" label became a cage that I decided I would no longer yield to.

It was that summer that I decided that I would take the necessary steps to rebrand myself. When I returned to school in August, I asked more questions in class. When group assignments were required, I made efforts to get to know my group members and to actively share my input. When encounters with fresh faces arose, I conversed. In many ways I forced myself to talk so that I could be heard; even if sometimes it created an uncomfortable internal situation.

It wasn't that I thought quiet was a bad thing. It was about proving to myself that I had the ability to become confident enough to express my inner thoughts, outwardly. It was about opening myself up to others and creating a bridge for cultivating potential relationships. It was about developing the strength to use my voice and understanding the power that my voice has. By no means am I a loud girl. But by all means I am a woman who speaks up for what she believes in. I am kind, yet direct. I am sweet, yet sincere. My voice is one of the most powerful tools I will ever sustain, and I plan to make the best possible use of it.

Safety Net

There is a fear that whirls around the unknown. As people we like to know what's next, so that we can properly prepare for the future. We protect ourselves in this way. When we don't feel like we can prepare or protect ourselves, it makes us uncomfortable. But what if I said we can protect ourselves even within the unknown? We can build our confidence in the area of uncertainty. We can do this with the knowing that no matter what happens we will always have the ability to keep pressing forward. We will always have another opportunity to create the reality or results that we are so hungrily seeking. And that is all the safety net we need.

I am

I am at a place that is neither here nor there
In between I've seen better days and extreme happiness
The stomping grounds of grateful but achievement is the goal
A little dark but mostly light
A little broken but mostly whole
A little sad but mostly happy

I try to live in the present—
But my mental wheels keep turning
Driving me to the past and the possibilities of the future
Bound only by the thoughts I allow to simmer
Into the flavor of my reality which are both hearty and yet, still
Leave me hungry.

And I think that's what a good cook does—
They create a meal so filling and desirable that
It fills you up but still leaves you wanting more.

And while I've never been a good cook in the kitchen
I've always been an immaculate chef of my thoughts
Whipping and stirring, flipping and turning heavy
thoughts into light fluffy ones.
Ones that I am delighted to consume, as they rest
In the pit of my belly and provide nutritional value to
the rest of my body,
Mind
And spirit.

I am thoughtful. I am thought full.

You won't always know *how* you will get there you just have to remember that you will.

Self-Reconciliation

For a long time, I was in denial about being an introvert. There was a part of me that was itching to always be outgoing and externally driven. It was the part of me that didn't want to get sweaty armpits when interacting with people. Do note, I said people and not *new* people which means that my pits get sweaty even when I chat with old friends. And this is not to say that this happens to all introverts but it for sure happens to this one.

I wanted to be an extrovert because they seem like so much damn fun. Like the life of the party. Like mingling with large groups of people every Friday and Saturday night. Like their social battery lives on for eternity or requires very little charging. And it's funny because I just stereotyped extroverts the same way that introverts are stereotyped. We are supposedly withdrawn and quiet. We are socially awkward and hate large groups of people. We're the wallflowers of the party and we do introvert things like read books or even write them.

Extroverts seemed like their lives were more opportunistic in the way of friendship, adventures, career opportunities and the lists go on. This is because it is no secret that society favors extroverts. Probably because they are natural-born people, people, which was certainly something that I wanted to identify with. I wanted to have fruitful friendships, exciting adventures and a career to be proud of. I think somewhere along the lines, I convinced myself that being an introvert was a weakness, a flaw, even. And I wanted to tuck that part of myself as deep down as possible, so that it couldn't hinder me in all the things I aspired to be and do.

Unfortunately, this tucking away was harmful. When the introvert in me needed to recharge its batteries, I would often spread myself thin by choosing to be around people despite my intense need for solitude. I've even beat myself up for not wanting to attend social gatherings that I was invited to. I wanted so badly to want to go but so often I simply didn't have the battery life to. And even worse is the guilt I felt for letting people who wanted me there, down. I'd often go anyway, to please others in addition to the part of me that wanted to align with extroversion.

I was on the track of losing myself before I had the self-actualization that being an introvert is as profound to my life journey as being a woman. Something that allows me to be receptive to the world around me could never be a weakness. A characteristic about my being that allows me to think deeply and create freely could never be a weakness. And the fact that I have a built-in timer that lets me know when I've had enough time around people and need to be alone is practically a superpower. Despite all of the stereotypes that we have about introverts and extroverts, we are all humans with needs that we must tend to. So, if that need is going out regularly with friends or if it's self-caring in the house on the weekends, we must do it. And even more importantly, we must be able to recognize the power of accepting ourselves in our entirety.

Quiet Ninja

The world will say things like "Do not dim your light to make others feel more comfortable in your presence." Yet in the same token the world says, "Be humble." I truly believe that these two ideas of being are conflicting. While I am not advocating oversized egos—I don't think that the term "humble" is quite as positive as some people make it out to be. If you don't believe me, Google the word *humble* and watch what the internet stirs up. The simple fact is people benefit from you most when you are being your authentic self. No bits and pieces required.

As of late, I have been intentional about the space that I take up and allowing my wings to stretch out as far as they wish to go. They are meant to be outstretched and not pinned to my sides so that others have more space to be comfortable. I am learning that there is enough space in the world for each of us; and more specifically, there is enough space in every room that I enter, to be myself in its entirety. That means to be myself in all of my wit, seriousness, humor, love, kindness and intellect. I am relearning that I am valid, not because others have confirmed that I am, but I am valid because I have chosen that for myself. There is nothing more wasteful than trying to measure up to the ideals that others do or don't have about me. In fact, I am learning not to take too intimately the words of others—as to be sure not to define myself by them.

I think of confidence as a quiet ninja. It's seldomly loud, but people always notice it. The issue is never confidence though, the issue is that people don't always like how confident people make them feel; which is only ever an issue when they lack confidence in some areas of their own life.

Doers

I can feel the words
Being forcefully pushed from my throat to my mouth
Like acid reflux.
Except these words don't sting
And they certainly aren't sour.
These are smooth and inviting
They are outspoken and sure of themselves
They are valid and give way to the
The wisdom of the mind behind them.

I have never claimed to be forthright or blunt
But I have also never been a stone-cold liar.
I'm good at describing things sweetly
Even words that should feel like fire.

I am straight to the point
Yet, my optimism is of the most supreme
I'm gifted with unwavering high spirits
And those are the wings that have carried me.

My wings are grand and colorful
There isn't a peak of sky that they cannot reach
They are muscular and sturdy
And resilient
And proud
And widespread
And cannot be clipped.

They soar over mountains and rivers, oceans and the abyss of
the unknown.
My wings are fearless and always full of wonder.
They're doers
And not sayers
And if they could say anything
They wouldn't.

I will not run from my fears. I will confidently face them.

A Letter to My Unborn Child: Part I

At some point this life will cease to exist and the only thing left will be the traces of crumbs that you left for the rest of the world to nimble on. Hopefully the crumbs that you leave will be full of nutrients and laughter, brilliant ideas and smiles. You only get to do this life once. That is why it is of the utmost importance to exercise your voice when needed. To stand up for what you believe in and to do everything it is, that you are afraid of.

The world is yours. And so is the universe and everything else in it. You are the most beautiful human being that has ever walked the face of this earth. In just your tiny body there is a soul that has power. Power to change minds, thoughts and lives. You are gifted with the ability to do each of those things. You are a gift to your father and I – the greatest one that we could have ever imagined.

You will be sensitive. It will hurt when you fall down in life. Just as it hurts when you fall while running on the playground, scraping your knees and elbows – but it will be worth it. Because the next time you fall down, it won't hurt half as bad. You will fail. Miserably. But your successes will greatly outweigh your failures; as a matter of fact, your successes will not be possible without your failures.

Be kind to those around you. The world is filled with enough ugly, do not contribute to its unattractiveness. Being kind is one thing that you will never regret but being ugly and mean is something you will one day wish you could take back.

Be a leader of your life, of your destiny and your generation. There is no one that knows you better than yourself. Even if your dad and I tell you that we do, it is not true. And you will spend your entire life trying to figure out exactly who you are, but you will know the entire time. Silly, right?

Never take anything too seriously. Like your dad, make serious moments humorous ones. It will carry you through the tough times. Embrace the tough times. They are not as bad as you think and they will only make you stronger, I promise.

Sometimes life will not make sense. Other times it will make the most sense. Do not spend time trying to decide which is which. Live, be free, smile and love. You are the most powerful creature birthed into this world.

Optimism is the ability to see light despite the inevitability of darkness.

Do What You Don't Want to Do

We live in a society that caters to the idea that we should not have to do something that we don't desire to do. While this is frequently acceptable and arguably even encouraged in some cases, this is not a feeling that we should consistently pursue. We should not journey through our lives avoiding everything that we don't desire taking action on. Generally, the things that we don't want to do are exactly the things that we need to do, in order to achieve the growth and results that we are eagerly seeking.

As you know by now, I am an introvert. While I enjoy spending time with people, I also require alone-time to recharge my batteries. I appreciate being at home because it is my refuge, but I am also naturally sociable. While I take pleasure in being alone, I require some sort of social interaction regularly, to feel my best. When invited to go out places with friends or family, I am often willing to go. And for every time I want to go, there is also a time that I don't. While I appreciate being included, I like to stay back in the comfort of my peaceful abode. However, it is imperative that I go out and spend time with friends and family regularly — because it is essential to my personal well-being. Sure, staying in the cozy warmth of my home watching movies would feel good, but it's something that I can do mostly any night and it won't always make me feel optimal. That's why it is critical that I push myself out of my comfort zone for a few hours and savor being out with the people I love. In the end, I'm always happy when I do.

Sure, introversion is my nature, but I still require that

interaction and most importantly connection with people. It provides me with a sense of belonging and love; both things that all humans require to nurture their well-being. Now for some, this belonging and love may not come in the form of spending time with friends or family. It varies for everyone, but whatever gives you that feeling, lean into it—even if you think you'd rather be doing something else. Because sometimes it's not about what you want to do but instead what you need to do, so that you can enjoy being the best version of yourself.

Living in My Truth

I finally learned what speaking my truth means and I don't think I can ever go back to my old ways of concealing my truth to soothe the hearts of other people. While I will never be the kind of person who spews out ugly truths every chance I get, I am not afraid to share ugly truths anymore. I am a firm believer in the power of truth no matter how painful it can be. The truth is light, and light is a necessity in having the ability to see clearly. Clear sight means clear vision which is necessary in the process of choosing a direction that we wish to move in.

Speaking my truth also means living inside of it and proclaiming it through body language. It means saying no to going out when I don't feel it in my soul to go out. It means respecting that I have needs, especially in terms of self-care and continually tending to those needs. Living in my truth means upholding the boundaries that I've set in my relationships. It means loving as hard as my heart desires and sharing my time wherever I believe it is most valuable. It means devoting my time where I feel most fulfilled. Living in my truth is so much larger than just speaking it. It is living in a way that feels best to me—a way that feels like warm fuzziness to my soul.

To My Quiet Parts

You were the fever I never wanted.
Always caught me by surprise
Sneaking up to my doorstep.
And although I knew you were invited to the party
I couldn't help but to think that the
Eucalyptus in my smile and the water in my spirit
Would be remedy enough to make you
Go away.

I wanted to drown you.

I didn't want to be the hero talking you down
From jumping off that bridge,
I wanted you to jump –
To end it.
I wanted to terminate the relationship I've had with
You all these years and yet…

Here you are.
The protagonist of my story.
The protector.
The healer.
The unwavering presence.

All pain will subside eventually. But the truth will last forever.

On Learning to Be Still

I am inspired to write this by a commercial that I just saw on TV. While I don't watch much TV, my husband often leaves it on a sports channel, in the living room and I can't help but to hear what's being said. The commercial that just played was about a dad having a pool built in his backyard and the takeaway message was "live your most fantastic life." And while that may be a very simple and direct message, it is such an important one. I'm sure that this message carries weight differently for each person, depending on their personal circumstances but what this message means for me is to remember to be present. To live in the moment. To *be still.*

Achievement has been a significant driver my entire life. I don't think this part of me will ever change nor am I seeking to change it. I enjoy aiming for higher and wanting to be the best version of myself. I am fired up by the personal satisfaction that I feel when I achieve a goal of mine — tremendous or tiny, because all goals matter.

However, the older I get the more I realize that so much of my life thus far has been lived revolving around a goal that I was working toward. While, I understand that this is precisely the way that achieving goals works, I've done it in the way of living in the future. Even today, I get ecstatic about planning and the things that are to come. There is so much joy and excitement in newness, which is what makes the future so enticing. The future is a fresh start, a clean slate, an unpainted canvas, a world of opportunity. And maybe that's why I am the person who LOVES Mondays! While so many people despise the start of a new week, I embrace it will full arms because I know it is sure to be filled with opportunities to project me forward in coming closer to my goals. Although, nowadays, I give myself breathing space. I stop and inhale and remember all that is. I take note of all of the blessings that I have in my life and how grateful I feel to have them.

My husband has helped me with this slowing down and stopping and smelling the roses. He probably doesn't know it, but he has. He helps me to realize that experiences and moments in time are invaluable — so I shouldn't fret about their monetary costs. He has helped me understand the importance of laughing and smiling in the small moments just as much as the big ones. He has challenged me to not sweat the small stuff (like him leaving his shoes everywhere or having a messy living room). He has indirectly taught me how to reevaluate my priorities, in the best possible way.

Being still and present are things that I know I will have to continue to work at throughout my entire life. I hope that one day they come as naturally to me as working toward achievement does.

28

The Waning

I am slowly diminishing old ways of thinking, knowing and being.

Angels

Sometimes it isn't the amount of time that you know a person that determines the depth of the impact. Sometimes it is the impact itself that determines the lasting depth they have on your life. Genuine people do not always come coated in the phrase "best friend." Sometimes they are wrapped in "something feels good about this." They have a way of penetrating the cracks in our lives that we had no knowledge existed and warming a spot in our hearts that we didn't know was cold. Each person who enters our life has something to give us and we enter the lives of others to do the same. May we never lose sight of the wisdom gained, the experiences felt and our obligation to pay it forward.

Forgiveness Part I: On Losing Friends

Looking back to my adolescent years, more specifically life before college—I had close-knit friends. I wouldn't call it a circle because, well not all of them were friends or even associated with each other. Each of them were my friends, individually. In hindsight it seems as though I made friends easily and seemingly really good ones.

It was not until the summer before my junior year of high school that I had a falling out with a good friend of mine. We used to hangout every day after school, beginning our sophomore year. She was a shyer and more reserved introvert while I was an introvert that was more outward and bubblier. I introduced her to a male friend of mine who was also an introvert. It was incredible to have a group of friends whose introversion I could relate to. We spent many late nights in her backyard having deep fulfilling conversations. She was perhaps the deepest thinker of us all. She internalized everything which made for fascinating dialogue. He was the jokester of the group that always kept us laughing with his witty and outrageous jokes. We were all writers too. We'd often exchange new poems that we'd written since the last time we'd seen each other. We definitely considered ourselves unusual and quite frankly, we were. We were unusual individuals but an even more unusual group. It seemed like we all had so much in common yet, brought so many different ideas and ways of thinking into the mix.

As our sophomore year came to an end, things began to change. I could tell that she and our male friend liked each other. The other kids on the block that we'd also hang out with from time to time and me, all knew this was coming. We were waiting for the day they'd begin dating. Neither of them would publicly display their affection though. They just flirted frequently. After I had gotten off work one weekend, I went over to her house to see if she was home and able to come outside. I checked the backyard first, because that's where she usually would be. And there she was, sitting on our male friend's lap on her patio in a white lawn chair. I felt intrusive and quickly apologized and left. All I could think to myself was "why wouldn't she tell me that they were dating or messing around?"

Fast forward a couple months. They began acting like they did not want me around. I caught onto this very quickly and tried my best not to show up where I was not wanted or appreciated. I ended up hearing directly from a mutual friend that she did not like me anymore. She mistook my bubbly, outward personality for having feelings for our male friend, which wouldn't work for her of course, since they liked each other. I didn't like him at all. That entire time we would all hang out together, I was talking to the man that is now my husband. I was completely invested in becoming my now husband's girlfriend. They were just my friends.

Shortly after I was called out of my name and unfriended. It was possibly one of the saddest moments of my life. Before this, I had never lost friends so close. These people knew so many things about me and some of the deepest parts of my life. I looked forward to hanging out with them every day. I felt like they really understood me. Instead though, they both viewed me as a threat to their relationship. It hurt because I had no bad intentions. I was actually rooting for them, but they just didn't see it that way. I think what was also hurtful is that we were a trio and to be the one ostracized was a reality that was hard to accept.

The summer before my junior year of high school I moved to Virginia. This meant a new school and new friends. I was so up for the journey, especially after what had just happened in my life. Interestingly enough, the following year she apologized to me for everything. I accepted her apology, but I knew things would never be the same. Especially since their relationship faltered and they didn't get far. I returned to Missouri for my senior year of high school. I couldn't hang out with both of them, because they despised each other and hanging out with them individually stirred up tension. I eventually stopped hanging out with either of them.

Senior year gave me enough time to heal and college would be a fresh start. I was grateful for this entire situation but only later when things became clear. In the beginning of my friendship with both of these individuals, I felt and saw red flags. Sometimes you know you are not particularly compatible with a person or people, but you make it work anyway, because once you reach a specific point, they become what is most familiar. And quite frankly, familiar feels a lot like being cuddled up in a soft blanket (burrito-style), while on top of a super comfy couch with the fluffiest pillows — while cold air blows into the room. You keep pretending that the red flags are flaws, and try to accept that everyone has them, since no one is perfect.

The reddest of flags that I experienced from both of them was their darkness that was divulged through their behavior and communication. Darkness is not something that should ever be overlooked. It didn't impair me

35

during our friendship because I brought balance. Instead of seeing it as a negative, I tried to learn and navigate their gloom by being open and understanding to this part of them. Unfortunately, my brightness became their annoyance. But soon enough, I learned that my brightness was not in vain and neither was their darkness.

In order to receive what we have asked the universe for we must be in a state that allows us to receive. This is one of open-mindedness, high spirits and a welcoming for change.

Realizations Part I: Learning, Relearning & Unlearning

It is such a beautiful thing when I have realizations about myself. The kind that come without the validation of others. The kind that no one has to tell me. Instead my highest being notifies me of these realizations; whispering them in my ear when I least expect it but need it most. Sometimes they are a treat – sweet like warm, freshly-risen cinnamon rolls. Other times these realizations are sour like lemonade without sugar. Both equally important.

Today *I learned*: that I am drawn to community. And that wherever I go in life, if there is not a sense of community, I create one. Connecting with others is an important part of myself. When I deny myself of this necessity, I create an imbalance within my being.

Today *I relearned*: that my spirits are naturally high. And that it is absolutely impossible for anyone to dim this shine about me. I came into this world with a set of lenses that not only believe but *know* that there is good everywhere and good in everyone.

Today *I unlearned*: that my soft, sweet nature is a bad thing. All too often people try to hide their softness. As though it is not vulnerability that makes them human. Like being soft is the equivalent of having no boundaries. They fail to remember that remaining soft in a world that praises being hard, takes guts, perseverance and intention. That being soft is not easy — that maybe being hard is far easier. Being sweet, is something that is simply engraved in my bones. It is how I allow myself to taste the small pleasures of life and to remain full of gratitude.

In order to break a cycle, you must first recognize that there is one.

Realizations Part II: I am Attracting Parasitic Friendships

As a natural giver I have a tendency to give my time, energy, love and wisdom to people who do not always appreciate it. I used to believe that it wasn't always necessary to be appreciated for giving those things — so long as I was giving out of sincerity and love. I am learning now though, that giving without getting, leads to feeling drained and resentful.

I don't usually expect people to reciprocate giving at the same intensity that I give, which could be a part of the reason I have been challenged to learn this lesson. What I do know for sure though, is that not everyone has the capability of reciprocation at the same level; even if they wish they could. This is something we must come to terms with if we aim to move into a space that doesn't include resentment. And while not everyone can reciprocate at the same intensity, it does not mean that we should avoid giving altogether.

Although not everyone is capable of reciprocating the same level of giving, everyone is perfectly capable of showing gratitude. This gratitude can come in the form of words or actions. When I do something for someone out of the kindness within my heart, I do anticipate gratitude to follow. The most inexpensive form of gratitude are the words "thank you" or "I really appreciate this." This form of gratitude is literally free. Maybe that's why I cannot wrap my head around why people don't ALWAYS show gratitude when someone has done something for them. When someone uses their time, energy or even money, to do something that benefits you, it deserves acknowledgement.

So, what do you do when you have a friend who is consistently unappreciative? Well, first things first, you may need to reevaluate the friendship. Ask yourself what makes you friends to begin with. As a person who places high value and expectation on gratitude for both myself and others, I find it difficult to have wholesome relationships with people who don't. This is because "when you don't have the same values, it is difficult to have a conducive relationship," as one of my wise friends once said. It is even more unlikely that the friendship will ever be meaningful for both people when the person who is incapable of reciprocation at the same intensity, is the same person who does not demonstrate gratitude.

I have faced this lesson many times in my life. But I never learned it until now. I never understood that the drained feeling after giving constantly without receiving in a friendship, is not healthy. I thought it was normal. I figured it was because maybe I had some soulful superpowers that could heal all who stepped foot in my presence. But each of these relationships played out the same way. I met them, became friends and gave so much time, energy and love; it felt filling and gave me a high because I felt a sense of purpose—as time went on, I began to feel drained, then the friendship ended. I finally understand that it should never get to the point of feeling drained.

Both people in any friendship should be making contributions—as close to equally as possible. And it isn't about measuring these contributions or trying to be fair. Of course, there will be times when one person is going through something like a heartbreak or bereavement and they will not be in an emotional state to have the ability to give which is acceptable. However, outside of these exceptions both parties should be pouring into each other's cups. The way to ensure that this happens in all of your friendships is to set boundaries. This means that your friend doesn't get to call you for the third time this week to vent to you without asking how you are doing. This means that your friend doesn't get to get away without saying thank you for the bill that you just paid after having coffee together. This means that the conversations that you have do not always get to be centered around them.

Boundaries can be difficult to set for existing friendships. Especially when the tone has already been set. But it is crucial if you are seeking balance in your life. Sometimes boundaries will be sitting down with a friend who you believe is worth keeping and telling them what you can no longer tolerate. Sometimes it's slowly pulling back from a friend that you were seeing red flags from anyway. It is especially making do's and don'ts very clear in new friendships so that what you will and will not tolerate is crystal clear.

Bliss

I can't say oblivion doesn't feel like bliss though,
Like rose petals smoothed across my cheeks
Like warm tea soothing my sore throat.
Oblivion was the home in which I lived for many years.
Until you saw it fit to break my windows, forcing me
To see a truth that did not light up my soul.
I am thankful for oblivion.
For its painlessness.
For its consideration as it
Attempts to shield us from a truth that is meant to
Harden us.
I am far more thankful for the truth though.
It is a reality that neither I nor my intuition can forever
avoid.
And while I appreciate the truth,
I am still learning how to love it.

To uplift others is to uplift yourself.

Self-Soothing: On Death

Everything has its end,
The flower's life
The hands we lend.

The stars grow dim,
Forever they won't last.
The life on earth we trim,
The end will be the past

For we cannot save the ends,
They come on their own.
It is like love that shatters,
And is then overthrown.

Why everything has an end,
Life may never know.
Or could it be its natural cycle
Embracing it to go?

Being a Victor of Growth

There is such a huge difference between feeling yourself growing and experiencing the results of growth. Feeling yourself grow feels a lot like being kicked in the kneecaps and pinched in the arm over and over again (sibling style). It's usually not the most pleasurable experience but as we all know, it is a necessary one. We may not always enjoy the process of growth, but we never complain about the result of it; when we get to sit back and admire the road we traveled and how much sturdier we've become.

In the midst of growth, it is imperative that we ask questions to ourselves that allow us to recognize the value of the process. Questions like, "how is this going to make me a stronger, more capable individual?" and "how is this moving me closer to becoming the best version of myself?" These questions empower us to be present in the moment and to take control of our perception of the events taking place during this growth process. These questions challenge us to remove the idea of being victims to the process and give us the power to become victors of the process.

Seeing ourselves as victors of the process helps us to adjust the lenses in which we see the challenge of growth. It allows us to face growth with open arms because while it isn't always easy, the results are always beautiful. It's significant for us to have positive, clear lenses to see growth through, for the simple fact that growth is a constant process in our earthly journey and if we shun the light in it, we will go mad from all of its ruggedness.

So instead of reminding ourselves that the storm will pass, the pain and discomfort of the growing will eventually subside—let us see the beauty in all of it while the storm is overhead. Let us take charge of our growth process while we are in it.

It is your own responsibility to motivate yourself and to keep pressing toward your dreams.

Things That Hold Us Back

I am the wall between
Your dreams, and all of which you fear —
I am the hammer that
Tears down your irretrievable mistakes
And the primer that coats your consciousness.
I am the battle between how tired you are
And how bad you really want it.
I am the production of your willpower
And the manifestation of your limitless thoughts.
I am the time it takes for you to comprehend
The benefit of self-discipline.
I am your lack of self-discipline.
I am all of the self-discipline that you wish you could have
But are too weak to achieve.
I am your silent doubter
Your inexistent "good luck charm"
Your inability to be mediocre.
I am your talent
I am the ambition in your smile
And the gorgeousness of you spirit.
I am the wall between
Your dreams and all of which you fear.

New Moon

52

I am still light.
Will always be light,
Shining through the day
And glowing through the night.
Even when you cannot see me.

Crossing the Bridge

Growing up I followed the straight and narrow path. Always doing the right thing and being the right thing. And of course, it sounds nice, until it's not.

From the very beginning of my life (and I'm talking kindergarten), I was driven by achievement. For a long time, I attributed this need for achievement to my strong sense of self-discipline and simply wanting to achieve it for myself. This is partially true. I wanted to achieve these things because I wanted to prove to *myself* that I could. And while, when I did it was nice to be congratulated by others — I knew that was not why I did it. The achievement through rewards and recognition was validation enough, or so I thought.

Achieving was about feeling wholeness. And I felt whole when I was constantly achieving. My achievements were louder than the internal turmoil that boiled inside of me. The ones that I tried my best to tune out, by staying on the move and continuously achieving.

Since graduating college, my life has changed immensely. One of the biggest changes is my current occupation. While writing this, I have a job that requires primarily silence, while focusing on one task at hand. Unfortunately, due to the circumstances of this job I am not able to disclose in detail what I do. But as a person who has always been on the move, I hope that you can imagine that this was initially torture. I could not fathom how people could work in an environment that left them idle with their thoughts for almost eight hours a day. In the beginning I saw this abundance of time to think to myself as a terrible idea. No distractions, no noise and very minimal conversation. Just me and these outrageous thoughts.

I have learned that silence allows for the truth to emit itself freely. It is in our silence that we learn our deepest truths. And sometimes that truth is not one that we thought we would ever have to face. One of my biggest, unwanted truths were that I required validation through the form of achievement. Achievements that I believed would build a reputation for myself, that others would gravitate to. A reputation that was tidy, golden and clean-cut. So much of my drive for achievement was personal, but it was also driven by the way that I believed other people should perceive me. The biggest mistake here was that I was allowing a large part of my identity to be defined by validation from sources outside of myself.

I've had to question my confidence and whether or not it ever existed. And if it did, could it stand tall and alone? I've had to question my ego and if it was made out of things that I told myself or things that others told me about myself. I've had to question who I am with zero outside validation and find a way to make myself feel whole within that space.

I won't lie, it has been a hard road since I have faced this daunting truth about myself. Some days have been uncomfortable, others more yielding, but this is a bridge I will continue to cross despite how shaky the path feels.

Optimism is the lit candle in the dark room of our lives. It is a way of thinking, feeling and living. And the truth is, there is an optimist inside of all of us. So instead of letting the realist in you take the wheel, let the optimist in you be the driver.

The Things We Hate Are Beautiful

It was the summer before our first year of college and my boyfriend of two years figured we should probably break up. It was a logical idea, considering I was going to college in North Carolina and he was going in Iowa. I think that's what most couples would've done – let the distance naturally separate them as they begin the journey of finding themselves and starting the rest of their lives in a completely different time zone.

I, however, could not let go of the fact that we had already survived long-distance for 11 months during our junior year of high school when I went to school in another state. Fortunately, I was able to return to my original high school for my senior year, but long-distance wasn't something that we anticipated undergoing in the future. Long-distance was inconvenient, sad and extremely difficult on our relationship, since we were just in the early stages. Some nights I would question whether the heartbreak of not seeing him on a daily basis was worth it. Not to mention the countless people who shed their own doubts about how long distance-relationships hardly ever work out.

We didn't listen to the naysayers. We both agreed to stay together despite being in different states for college. The biggest challenge was our first semester of college when we were exposed to an array of people of the opposite sex. As a human, it is natural to notice attractive people. In a long-distance relationship, it is dangerous to notice and interact with attractive people. Unfortunately, we weren't together on a regular basis to reinforce what we had right in front of us. We would Skype and talk on the phone in between classes and at night but the longing for physical touch almost became a deal-breaker. That first semester felt like we crumbling as a couple. We began talking less and became more deeply involved in the separate lives that we'd created. It took a toll on my heart, since he was my high school love and I'd known him since we were just 12. It was becoming evident that our relationship was no longer providing the strength, love and support that a relationship should. We had drifted so far apart, the odds of things ever being the same again, weren't looking good.

We decided to take a break at the end of that first semester; which is generally code for "breaking up, but we're going to do this as slowly and nicely as possible." The break was everything we needed during that time. During that break I rediscovered who I was without him. I remembered that my world didn't begin or end with him. I am whole, entirely on my own. I used the extra time to get involved in clubs and organizations on campus that filled me with joy. I hung out with genuine people that made me feel connected with them. I decided that our break would likely be permanent. I wished him well, but this chapter of my life had to be about pouring into and loving on myself.

After two weeks of our break he asked if he should still fly to see me during winter break, like we had agreed on pre-break. I told him that it would not be necessary since we were simply friends. I actually told him not to come. I didn't want to revisit fresh wounds during a time that I should be recovering from homework assignments, tests and finals week. Him being the stubborn human being that he is, surprised me and came anyway. I can't say I was upset. Seeing his face felt like the closure I might need.

He stayed for just a few days. We enjoyed each other's company, but things felt awkward in comparison to before the first semester of college. I still loved him deeply. But not enough to sacrifice the mission I was on to focus on myself and the direction of my own life. The night before New Year's Day we decided that we would go into the new year as a couple no longer on a break. I told him this was the last stab at it, that I was willing to take. If we needed another break, we needed not to be together.

Six semesters and six months of living together, later, he became my husband. For the rest of our long-distance relationship we learned to find our groove. Which meant taking turns flying to see each other and having designated times when we would chat or FaceTime. Every time one of us left the other to fly back home, it was difficult, but it got easier, because we could vividly see the long-distance journey coming to an end.

Now that I've moved to Missouri where my husband is, I am in a long-distance relationship with my sisters and family. Long-distance is not something I will ever get used to doing with the people that I love. However, I will say I am definitely more equipped this time around.

No More Safekeeping

I do not pity myself
For my losses, shortcomings or lack thereof
I realized years ago, that pity only amounts to
Complacency and a heaping pile of sadness
And to be quite honest,
Sad isn't my favorite emotion.
Instead of pity though, I allow myself to feel whatever is
troubling me — fully.
I take it in the same way I inhale a deep breath.
I exhale it too.
Because that is the natural thing to do.
Not to harbor it for safekeeping
Because if sad were a person, she wouldn't want to be
kept safe.

Walking Away Has Served Me Well

"Go where you are celebrated—not tolerated. If they can't see the real value of you, it's time for a new start."
~Unknown

Being celebrated means being surrounded by people who love who you are, who see all of your potential and help you celebrate your successes. Being celebrated is being around people who enjoy your energy, who appreciate your talent and who always leave room for you at the table.

I remember seeing this quote as a signature at the closing of one of my professor's emails. It was my junior year of college and I couldn't help but to be taken back by how much truth that quote holds. At the time, the quote resonated with me in a differently than it does today, but nonetheless I find periods of time in my life where this quote pushes its way to the forefront of my mind; like a reminder that I need to walk away from things that are serving me poorly.

Sometimes this means a friendship, other times it might be a job. The thing that is so detrimental about being where you are tolerated instead of celebrated is that you are not where you belong. And believe me, you know if you are not where you belong. You'll feel it in your gut and maybe even deep in your soul. If you're like me, you'll see red flag after red flag because you tried to ignore the first red flag. But please listen to me when I say those red flags are there to guide you *away* from what you need. Yes, sometimes life works in a way that does not point to where we should go, but instead where we shouldn't; which ultimately leads us to where we should be.

I have walked away from numerous relationships, jobs and situations where I was simply tolerated. I wasn't celebrated because I wasn't appreciated for all that I am. In some relationships my generosity was not appreciated but instead became expected, leaving me feeling hurt and resentful. With several jobs, my optimism, kindness and friendly nature was not celebrated. I am almost sure there were times when it was frowned upon and therefore, tolerated. With the combination of that and not being able to use my skills and talents, I knew that it was time for a new start. Sometimes it's as simple as reading how the energy in the room is cohesive with yours. When your energy is continuously out of sync with those in that space, it is likely that you will only ever be tolerated.

Being around people and in spaces where you are celebrated, allow you to be your best self. Therefore, it is our responsibility to remove ourselves from relationships, jobs and situations where we are tolerated and to involve ourselves in situations where we are undoubtedly celebrated.

There is a difference between doing work that you are good at and work that you love. May you find work where both of these characteristics coexist.

Work you Love is More Important Than a Paycheck

Paychecks help you live. Doing work that you love keeps you alive. After recently leaving a job that depleted my energy, leaving me feeling sad and depressed, I began working at a job that in its own right is a million times better. I finally work in a professional office-setting that keeps me busy all day long. Since I work in customer service again, my colleagues are generally friendly and helpful. For the first time in my life I have my own desk at work. That might seem like a small thing but when I first got my desk and desk key (yes, it locks!), I was more excited than you can imagine. Starting something new is always exciting! Then eventually, like most things, the excitement wears off and things become repetitive.

This is likely to happen during the course of most jobs, unless, you're doing work that you love and are whole-heartedly passionate about it. Things don't get dull when you're doing work that you love. Things may become challenging and cause frustration, but they don't lose their brilliance or power.

Transitioning into this new job is something that I had to do for my mental, emotional, physical and spiritual well-being. This new job has replenished energy that I lost working at my previous job. Here, I feel like I get to be a little more of myself. Most importantly, I don't get a stomach ache before my shift, like I used to at my old job.

However, working at my new job for just the short month that I have been there, has reaffirmed that having several businesses of my own is the ultimate goal. Having a conventional job has never been my style and isn't something I can see myself doing long-term. I have the self-discipline, drive and dedication to work for myself, so why wouldn't I? When I was twelve, my dream was to have a cupcake shop and to own a book publishing company — not to climb the corporate ladder. What is exceedingly important though, is that we enjoy and love whatever it is that we do. The world needs people who are passionate about the work that they invest their time into; because when people are passionate about what they do, we all benefit.

Gratitude

I am grateful for challenges and the wisdom they have afforded me. I am grateful for the wisdom that I am afforded by people who willingly share their experiences in the hope that it helps someone else. I am grateful for the people who are genuinely kind because they feel only kindness deep within themselves; the people who are kind to others and most importantly kind to themselves. I am grateful for people who have shown up for me in my life even during the times I would not have had the ability to show up for them; for the people who've shown up for me without any expectation. I am grateful for the highest of highs that I've experienced in my lifetime — the ones that kept me dreaming and soaring and expecting only goodness from the world. I am grateful for the lows that challenged me to find a coping mechanism that would pull me up again; I am grateful for the lows because as cliché as it may sound, they taught me how good the highs feel.

I am grateful for the infinite universe of knowledge, the one that I have the opportunity to explore each and every day. The new skills I've acquired from it, the ideas I have developed from it and the things I have been able to implement in my own life from its vastness and abundance. I am grateful for Mother Nature and the love that she showers us with daily by providing all the things that we need to survive despite the destruction that we knowingly cause her. She is the epitome of healing and forgiveness — of love and light, beauty, kindness and balance.

I am grateful for time. The way that it ends things and starts new things — the way it tattoos experiences onto our hearts and pushes us to be still in the moment, because even this moment is already gone.

A Letter to my Unborn Children: Part II

I used to think about being a mother more frequently in my teenage years. I specifically remember having the same dream multiple times where I was dressed in a long white flowy dress, sitting on a wooden swing in my backyard with a belly that had to have been at least 8 months along. I swung back and forth as the wind blew through my hair and you kicked your little feet inside my belly. I felt angelic. I knew that one day I would be gifted with the task of being a mother to a child that is nothing short of perfect. I thought about it probably more than most people my age. I knew though, that I didn't want to be a teenage mom. While there is nothing wrong with being a teenage mom, I have always been a person who likes to prepare for things. I knew that being a mom was a task that would take YEARS to prepare for. I wanted being a mother to be very intentional and I still do today. So, until I become your mother, I will be sure to collect as much knowledge and wisdom as possible, so that I can make sure you are equipped with the tools necessary to navigate and enjoy life.

As of lately, I have been thinking about what kind of mother I want to be. And what I've learned is this: I want you to feel cared for every moment you take a breath and during every challenge that you hurdle through. I want you to feel like I am there for you past the whirlwind of adolescence and into the reality of adulthood. I want you to know that even when you've surpassed the age of 50, I am still your mother and I still love you the way I did the moment you made your grand entrance into the world.

I imagine that loving your children is sort of like

learning to ride a bicycle. Sure, it's nice if someone shows you how to do it; it is preferred. But if someone doesn't show you how to, it doesn't mean that you are incapable of riding the bike. It just means that you'll have to learn it for yourself. You might fall more frequently and scrape those knees of yours, or maybe you won't. The important thing is that you get on that seat and push those pedals.

That is precisely what I plan to do when I am your mother. I will be your listening ear. Your confidant (as long as you will allow me to be so). I will give you space to bloom and grow into yourself the way my parents allowed me to. However, I will never let you forget or wonder if I am in your corner. I will always make myself available to have meaningful conversations or to just crack a laugh. I will enlighten you with stories that have taught me how to be strong, loving and grateful. When you leave for college, I will visit you a few times a semester and I will have regular check ins with you. I will love you even from afar, but I will never allow you to feel like we are far away in relationship to each other.

As your mother, I will still be growing and learning, and I will always remind you of that. I will remind you that I am human, the way you are and that I make mistakes the same way you do. I will never pretend to be perfect and I will never pressure you to feel like you have to be either. I know that being your mom will be one of the greatest hats I'll wear in this lifetime; I know that it will give me a new-found sense of purpose; I know that with and through you I will experience a kind of love like no other. I am not your mother yet, but I will be once you read this—and I am already proud of you.

Advice isn't always universal. We must be able to distinguish when it is useful and applicable to our own lives and equally when it isn't.

Social Media Detox

In this information era where we consume information at a rate higher than ever and in such abundance, we have to keep in mind that it is unnatural. Social media has enabled us to adapt to this era with ease, but our minds still require a break.

For so many free moments in the day, I have my head down in my phone, swimming through a vortex that doesn't always serve me well. Now, I do believe social media platforms are useful. They are genius-created and allow the world to connect socially. Although, as a creative, social media can be a hindrance to authenticity of thought. When we are constantly consumed with social media it can be difficult to decipher our own thoughts and ideas. Sure, inspiration is wonderful. But we have to allow ourselves the ability and space to inspire ourselves. To create without anything influencing us—if we can help it. This is where originality comes from when art is created.

One of my newly adopted practices is being off all social media mediums two hours before bed, as well as not checking any social media platforms until after two hours of being awake. I originally thought this was going to be a challenge, but it has been surprisingly easy and is such a breath of fresh air. Not only have I taken control of my social media use, I have minimized it significantly by making the window of using it, smaller.

Another practice that I have implemented is detoxing from social media at least once every two weeks and more frequently as needed. These detoxes last anywhere from 2-5 days depending on how much of a getaway I feel that I need. I usually choose to detox when I am looking to be more productive on a specific project, when I feel like I've become oversaturated with information and or when my spirits are a bit down. When my spirits are down is possibly the most important time for me to detox from social media, because social media tends to be a place where we subconsciously compare ourselves to others, which can be incredibly harmful.

It is difficult to think about my life without Instagram and other social media platforms. Especially since it is a way for me to connect with the world at any moment, wherever I am. And while social media has filled up so much time in my day to day life, I'm not advising that we eliminate it from our lives altogether. This is the era that we live in and social media has become a noteworthy tool. What I do believe though, is that we must recognize it as a tool and not a necessity in life. And every so frequently, it's imperative that we detox and reboot.

Consistency is powerful.

Human

I am convinced
That to feel everything deeply
Is a far better burden than
To feel nothing at all.
To avoid emotions — in a way that
Actions do not erupt a reaction
In your fanny pack of feelings
Or your tightly sealed miniature box of meltdowns
Is beyond unsettling.
To be human is to experience emotions
To have emotions may mean being an emotional
wreck—
And who wouldn't want to take a hammer to the
drywall
Every once in a while?

Forgiveness Part II: On Losing Friends

Perception is a reflection of how we feel on the inside. While I may have "lost" a few close friends in my lifetime I have gained an immense amount of wisdom and insight through those losses. In fact, I have gained far more than I've lost in the process...

I have gained peace of mind and heart, and a better understanding of what I seek in a friendship as well as what I don't.

I have learned where and when boundaries should be set.

I have learned the value of being truthful despite how your friend may feel about the truth.

I have learned that friends have your best interests at heart, and if a person does not—they are not your friend no matter how convenient the friendship is.

I have learned that you do not have to have all of the same opinions in a friendship, but it is imperative that each person respect the other person's opinion at the very least.

I have learned that friendship is a give and take, both of which should be done as equally as possible.

I have learned to be upfront in my friendships the same way I want my friends to be upfront with me.

Through my losses of friendship, I have learned how to be a better friend and a better human. I deeply

75

understand the importance of transparency and vulnerability. While I think I was a good friend before, I believe I am an even better friend now, because of what I've journeyed through.

Intention is important, but so is the result of your intention. We are not measured by good intentions but rather by good results.

Mediocrity Is Not in Your Bones

Stop. Wherever you are in life, just stop and take a moment to acknowledge that you surpassed challenges that often felt impossible. That you allowed yourself to see the silver lining even when it didn't seem logical. Acknowledge that you have continued to press forward despite the storms that you've traveled through. Stop and acknowledge that your strength is incredible. That your determination is unmatched and that your life is significant. No matter where you've been, where you are or where you will go, you are special. No one has to tell you this for it to be true, you have to know that it is. Whether you're in a hard place or a great one; whether you feel accomplished or are in the process of furthering your accomplishments...understand that while you are driven, motivated, ambitious and hard-working – you are also successful, generous, loving and entirely beautiful. The world could definitely use a couple more YOUs.

Cheers to all of the new beginnings you will create and all of the ones that will create themselves. Do not get ready for them, be ready.

80

Made in the USA
Monee, IL
04 December 2019